D0862651

The Science of Prophecy

by Dr. E. Bernard Jordan

The Science of Prophecy
(Formerly *Prophets of God's Kingdom*)
ISBN 0-939241-07-2

www.bishopjordan.com

PREFACE

God is raising up a people who will speak His will without compromise. He wants a voice that will cry out, even as John the Baptist cried out.

> *"As it is written in the prophets, Behold, I send my messenger before thy face, which shall prepare thy way before thee.*
> *The voice of one crying in the wilderness, Prepare ye the way of the Lord, make his paths straight."*
>
> — Mark 1:2-3

Before God makes any major move, He will always send forth a Moses or a John the Baptist; a prophetic voice to speak His Word.

God will speak His Word into the earth by a man or woman who will yield themselves unto Him. He will use someone who is not moved by people's faces or by the devil. A people who will not become fainthearted or disarrayed at what is happening around them, about them, or in the land.

God is looking for a people who will come before His throne with boldness. He is looking for a people through whom He can freely flow, as free as a drop of blood flows through one's veins, uninhibited by nothing.

Moses said on one occasion, *". . . would God that all the Lord's people were prophets, and that the Lord would put His Spirit upon them!"* (Numbers 11:29).

God has always had someone through whom He could communicate His Word.

I Peter 2:9 says, *"But ye are a chosen generation, a royal priesthood, an holy nation, a peculiar people; that ye should show forth the praises of him who hath called you out of darkness into marvelous light."*

God is looking for a people who will display His glory in the earth . . . a Kingdom of people who will utter His Will in the earth.

Jesus prayed:

> *". . . Our Father which art in heaven, Hallowed be thy name.*
> *Thy kingdom come. Thy will be done in earth, as it is in heaven.*
> *Give us this day our daily bread.*

And forgive us our debts, as we forgive our debtors.

And lead us not into temptation, but deliver us from evil: For thine is the kingdom, and the power, and the glory, for ever. Amen."

— Matthew 6:9-13

In verse 10, Jesus said, "Thy kingdom come. Thy will be done in earth, as it is in heaven." God's Will is already established in heaven. We are to pray that His Will and purpose be done in the earth.

I challenge you to obey the call God has placed upon your life. Open your ears up to hear what God is saying unto you this day, for the winds of God's Spirit are once again blowing upon His prophets. They have awakened out of their slumber. They have shaken themselves. They have put on the battle garments and are ready for war.

There is an arising of a mighty army ready for battle, and they will walk together as one: one people, one nation, one body, and one voice in the Lord.

They shall speak the same thing in love and in demonstration of the Holy Ghost. They shall speak prophetically. They shall prophesy and prophesy without end. They shall speak as the mouthpiece of God. Mighty and powerful shall they be, for they shall display the uncompromised Word of God.

A new dawn is arising. A company of prophets is arising who will have a knowing and an understanding of the times. They will have an understanding of the manifold wisdom of God, and they will express it throughout the land. All shall stand in amazement as the systems of this world become dismantled by the power of the Holy Ghost. The sons of God are maturing into the fullness of Christ.

Truly the sun is getting brighter and brighter! Praise the Lord! Hallelujah!

— Debra Jordan

The Science of Prophecy is dedicated to Aaron Bernard Jordan, who is called to maintain the legacy of his father, and carry the prophetic mantle throughout the earth in his generation.

In Gratitude

We'd like to give the following individuals a special thank you for their faithfulness and support in helping to make our dream come true:

Tijuana Baylor
Pastor James & Donna Duncan & Family
Pastor Richard Eberiga
Annette Giles
Dr. Carolyn Harrell
Elder Fitzgerald A. King
Pastor Connie Miles
Judy I. Ownby
Belinda Taylor
Alfreda Turner
Dianne M. Vincent
Prophetess Connie Williams

Because of their generosity and obedience to the Spirit of God, we know that they have opened the door for miracles, and we believe that He shall cause the gems of wisdom that are contained within these pages to be made manifest in each of their lives, for the reward of the Lord is sure and addeth no sorrow!

In His Love and Service,
Bishop E. Bernard & Pastor Debra Jordan

TABLE OF CONTENTS

INTRODUCTION

There is a vast difference between a person who speaks a prophetic word and one who is anointed, appointed, and ordained to the governmental office of a Prophet or Prophetess.

There is a way to discern the prophet of God from the prophet of Baal — or the genuine from the counterfeit.

The role of the prophet must be accepted and respected so that every member of the Body of Christ may find his or her place and step into position in God's army. God spoke to my heart, "My Body shall *not* be out of joint."

There is some growing and understanding that must take place for each member of God's army to step into proper position — and some of that growing must be in understanding, accepting, and re-specting the office of the Prophet, as well as the other governmental offices which Christ Jesus Himself set in the church — His Church.

Practical truths of the office of the prophet are unveiled in this book which I believe will be of benefit to those called to the governmental office of the prophet as well as the layperson in better understanding his supportive role of this office.

Chapter 1

REALMS OF PROPHETIC GIFTS

In I Corinthians 12, four different levels of prophecy are presented. As we become more familiar with these levels of prophecy, I believe it will remove the intimidation you may have concerning prophetic mysteries and ministries.

Many churches and individuals do not recognize the realm of prophetic ministry in which they are functioning. I believe our Heavenly Father wants to bring clarity in this area so that the entire Body of Christ might become unified, hence effective and triumphant in this final hour of the church age.

The four realms of prophetic gifts are:

— Manifestation of Prophecy
— Grace Gift of Prophecy
— Spirit of Prophecy
— The Office of the Prophet

1

Manifestation of Prophecy

Paul speaks of the manifestation of prophecy in I Corinthians 12.

> *"Now concerning spiritual gifts [or the things of the Spirit, or the spirituals], brethren, I would not have you ignorant."*
>
> Verse 1

The word for gift in the Greek language is PNEUMATIKOS. We could read verse 1, "Now concerning the PNEUMATIKOS (the things of the Spirit), brethren, I would not have you ignorant."

The "spiritual gifts" Paul is referring to are actually manifestations of the Spirit rather than gifts of the Spirit.

When you receive the Holy Spirit, you receive all of the manifestations of the Spirit. They are dwelling on the inside of you.

Paul did not want the church at Corinth to be ignorant concerning spiritual manifestations. He says in verse 2:

> *"Ye know that ye were Gentiles, carried away unto these dumb idols, even as ye were led."*

A dumb idol is anything that is void of the voice of the Lord. If you are following a man who does not have God's voice and he is not speaking the oracles of God, he is a dumb idol. I believe many people in churches today are being led by dumb idols — by men and women who are void of the voice of the Lord.

"Wherefore I give you to understand, that no man speaking by the Spirit of God calleth Jesus accursed: and that no man can say that Jesus is the Lord, but by the Holy Ghost."

Verse 3

Therefore, in any manifestation of the Holy Spirit, you are presenting the Lordship of Jesus Christ. That can only be done by the Holy Ghost.

"Now there are diversities of gifts, but the same Spirit."

Verse 4

The word gifts in verse 4 is CHARISMA, which refers to grace gifts. Paul is saying, "There are diversities of CHARISMA, but the same Spirit."

"And there are differences of administrations, but the same Lord."

Verse 5

Administrations refer to governmental ministries — the Apostle, Prophet, Evangelist, Pastor, and Teacher. There are different administrations (different offices), but it is the same Lord, which is Jesus.

"And there are diversities of operations, but it is the same God which worketh all in all.

> *"But the manifestation of the Spirit is given to every man to profit withal."*
>
> Verses 6-7

Paul then lists the manifestations of the Spirit.

> *"For to one is given by the Spirit the **word of wisdom;** to another the **word of knowledge** by the same Spirit;*
> *"To another **faith** by the same Spirit; to another the **gifts of healing** by the same Spirit;*
> *"To another the **working of miracles;** to another **prophecy;** to another **discerning of spirits;** to another **divers kinds of tongues;** to another the **interpretation of tongues:"***
>
> Verses 8-10

Then Paul says:

> *"But all these worketh that one and the self-same Spirit, dividing to every man severally as he will."*
>
> Verse 11

In other words, the Holy Spirit will divide the gifts according to the will of the Father or according to the need He sees in a church. The Holy Spirit distributes severally as He wills.

Kathryn Kuhlman is a beautiful example of someone moving in the manifestations of the Spirit. Often in her meetings she would have the congregations worship the Lord, bringing the audience into an atmosphere of reverence to the Holy Spirit, building an expectation to see the manifestation of the Spirit as she waited upon Him. She tapped into learning how to move in the manifestations of the Spirit.

She coveted earnestly the best gifts or the best things that were needed at a specific time. She possessed the Holy Spirit, and she moved in the manifestations of the Spirit. This, of course, can be done by any believer in the Body of Christ. The manifestations are not reserved for governmental ministries. Any believer can move in the manifestations of the Spirit.

The manifestation of prophecy is a manifestation of the Holy Spirit for the threefold purpose of edifying, exhorting, and comforting.

> *"But he that prophesieth, speaketh unto men to edification, and exhortation, and comfort."*
> I Corinthians 14:3

The manifestation of prophecy where the Word of the Lord flows will bring edification, exhortation, and comfort unto men. Edification means "to build up." Exhortation means "to admonish or to warn." Comfort means "to console."

Grace Gift of Prophecy

Another level of prophecy is what we call "the grace gift of prophecy" or the office of prophecy.

> *"For as we have many members in one body,*

and all members have not the same office:
   "So we, being many, are one body in Christ,
and every one members one of another.
   "Having then gifts [or having the CHA-
RISMA] differing according to the grace that is
given to us, whether prophecy, let us prophesy
according to the proportion of faith;
   "Or ministry, let us wait on our ministering:
or he that teacheth, on teaching;"
Romans 12:4-7

Notice that teaching is mentioned in verse 7. I believe there is a grace gift of a teacher, and there is a governmental gift of a teacher. The anointing, however, is different upon each of these teaching gifts.

You could have an individual who is moving in a grace gift of teaching, ministering to the church possibly in the area of the Sunday School. Yet, this person will not function in the governmental structure of the church as a teacher. We must recognize that there is a difference between those who function in various levels of service and those who are elders of the church. Everyone who teaches in the church of the Lord Jesus Christ will not necessarily be an elder.

There are others who will never be elders. Perhaps their lives are out of order. They are moving by a grace gift of teaching, yet the office of the teacher is not functioning because they have not been separated to function in the governmental structure of the church.

A person may be gifted to teach, but this does not mean that he is eldership potential. It's the same way with the office of prophecy or the grace gift of prophecy and the office of the prophet.

You may have an individual in your church who can prophesy, but who is not ready to move into the governmental aspect of eldership as a prophet in the church. The individual can tell you what God is saying, but he cannot bring sound counsel and wisdom for the steering of the church.

I believe there are a lot of people pastoring churches who really aren't pastors. They are moving by a grace gift of ruling, but the office of pastor is not present and people are being blessed.

You can have an individual whose marriage is all messed up, but there is an anointing on his (or her) life. When you hear his tapes or when he/she prophesies, you receive something from him/her. I believe this person is functioning by a grace gift, but the Doma gift (the office of the prophet) is not there. A person is not a prophet in the local church house until such a person has been recognized by the eldership of the Body and his ministry has been proven. I believe his ministry will be proven on the level of the grace gift before he enters into the Doma gift.

God does not change His mind concerning your gift or your calling. "For the gifts and calling of God are without repentance" (Romans 11:29). However, it is up to you to prove or work out that which is in you and bring it into manifestation.

Remember, Romans 12:6 says, *"Having then gifts differing according to the grace that is given to us. . . ."* Grace is that which you have not even merited. Someone once said, "Grace is God's riches at Christ's expense."

You receive your gifts according to God's grace. Before the foundation of the earth, God knew there was something He was going to impart in each of you. He imparted different levels of gifts.

The second half of Romans 12:6 says, *". . . whether prophecy, let us prophesy according to the proportion of faith."* In other words, a prophetic word or the prophecy that we might give will be delivered according to the degree of faith that is in us, or to the degree of Word that is in us, because faith cometh by hearing the Word of God (Romans 10:17).

The level of your Word knowledge will also determine the strength of your word, and the level of your understanding of the Scriptures will determine the type of prophetic flow that comes through you.

Romans 12:7 and 8 continue:

"Or ministry, let us wait on our ministering: or he that teacheth, on teaching;
"Or he that exhorteth, on exhortation. . . ."

The New Testament evangelist is to *strengthen the church.* The evangelist's ministry is not for the sinner. It is for the church. It is the believers who are to go out and do the work of the ministry, but it is the evangelist who brings the glad tidings of Jesus Christ and exhorts the church.

Many evangelists are moving by a great gift of exhortation. They are not New Testament evangelists, nor are they moving in the governmental ministry of an evangelist for they are to perfect the Saints, not perfect the sinners. As part of the five-fold ministry, they are to perfect the Saints for the work of the ministry.

Verse 8 of Romans 12 continues, *". . . he that giveth, let him do it with simplicity. . . ."* There is a grace gift of giving. *". . . he that ruleth, with diligence. . . ."* There is also a grace gift of ruling.

An individual could be a good ruler. A lot of churches have rulers, but they lack the gift of pastor. There is a big difference.

Then there are some churches that are being won by Madison Avenue techniques — not by the heart of a shepherd. They are functioning by a grace gift, but the governmental aspect of Christ is not there in the church.

Prophecy in verse 6 means "to see, to have the ability to see into, or to be able to see something beforehand." You can have a great gift of prophecy and you can be very predictive, but that does not mean you are a Prophet.

We must ask ourselves a question. What foundation or revelation did this person bring to the church? You see, the church is built upon the foundation of the Apostle and the Prophet of which Jesus Christ is the Chief Cornerstone. A Prophet doesn't just speak a word into this one's life and that one's life. *A person operating in the office of a prophet must be able to communicate the purpose of the Lord to the church.*

When you have an individual moving in the grace gift of prophecy who does not have an anointing upon his life to be a Prophet and he is trying to lay a foundation in the church, he begins to flow in flaky revelation. Often this person will try to force something or introduce something that simply is not there.

I believe the thing we will begin to see is that the Prophet will begin to show us a lot of things which are really out of order. In other words, a lot of things that we have been calling God are not God!

The Spirit of Prophecy

Now the spirit of prophecy works very similar to the manifestation of prophecy. We get the term "spirit of prophecy" from Revelation 19:10.

"And I [John] fell at his feet to worship him. And he said unto me, See thou do it not: I am thy fellowservant, and of thy brethren that have the

*testimony of Jesus: worship God: **for the testimony of Jesus is the spirit of prophecy.***"

The spirit of prophecy is whatever thing you hear from the Father that gives testimony to Jesus.

In Numbers 11:24-29, when there was a transference of spirits, one of the things that happened was they all began to prophesy.

> "*And Moses went out, and told the people the words of the Lord, and gathered the seventy men of the elders of the people, and set them round about the tabernacle.*"
> "*And the Lord came down in a cloud, and spake unto him, and took of the spirit that was upon him, and gave it unto the seventy elders: and it came to pass, that, when the spirit rested upon them, they prophesied, and did not cease. [It was like a spirit of prophecy swept over the place.]*"
> "*But there remained two of the men in the camp, the name of the one was Eldad, and the name of the other Medad: and the spirit rested upon them; and they were of them that were written, but went not out unto the tabernacle: and they prophesied in the camp.*"
> "*And there ran a young man, and told Moses, and said, Eldad and Medad do prophesy in the camp.*"
> "*And Joshua the son of Nun, the servant of Moses, one of his young men, answered and said, My lord Moses, forbid them.*"
> "*And Moses said unto him, Enviest thou for my sake? **would God that all the Lord's peo-***

ple were prophets, and that the Lord would put
his spirit upon them!"

In other words, Moses was encouraging the
people to prophesy, and this is what every Pastor
needs to do. Again, however, just because a person
prophesies doesn't mean he is moving in the governmental aspect of the office of a Prophet. We need
to understand that with clarity. I don't care if
Brother So-and-so prophesies twice every week.
That doesn't mean that he is a Prophet.

We read about a company of Prophets in I Samuel 10:9-13.

> *"And it was so, that when he had turned his
> back to go from Samuel, God gave him another
> heart: and all those signs came to pass that day.*
>
> *"And when they came thither to the hill, be-
> hold, a company of prophets met him; and the
> Spirit of God came upon him, and he prophesied
> among them.*
>
> *"And it came to pass, when all that knew him
> beforetime saw that, behold, he prophesied among
> the prophets, then the people said one to another,
> What is this that is come unto the son of Kish? Is
> Saul also among the prophets?*
>
> *"And one of the same place answered and said,
> But who is their father? Therefore it became a
> proverb, Is Saul also among the prophets?*
>
> *"And when he had made an end of prophesy-
> ing, he came to the high place."*

We can see that Saul, by coming into the School

of the Prophets or into the company of the Prophets, prophesied. Seeing a need in the Body of Christ and trying to meet it does not mean you have the call or the anointing to do so. We need to discern the difference between seeing a need and having a call.

I heard one man explain it this way. "You can be around the source for so long that you have the flavor of it, but you don't have the meat."

I believe Saul got into the flavor of prophecy, but he wasn't a Prophet. He did not have a Prophet's ministry. This is comparable to putting a banana in the refrigerator. The milk, the orange juice, and even other foods absorb the flavor of that banana. However, just because you drink milk that tastes like a banana does not mean it is a banana!

If you are around a strong prophetic ministry and you go to another man's house, most people won't even know the difference, especially if they haven't had revelation or illumination. They will say, "You are a Prophet." The flavor is there, but they aren't receiving the real thing. They are a blessing to the Body of Christ, they are helping in the church, we get blessed when they prophesy, but they do not have the governmental aspect of the office to bring steering and direction into the church. There are boundaries within their ministries. We must discern the flavor from the contents or substance.

I know of a particular church where the Pastor and his wife move in tongues and interpretation.

Nearly every couple in their church flows in tongues and interpretation just like the Pastor and his wife. Why is this? Because the spirit of the leader has come upon the congregation, and they flow under that mantle.

I remember a certain group of people whose tongues rhymed when they prophesied. Everyone who came out of that local church prophesied in rhyme, because that was the flavor that was mixed into that house. There are different prophetic modes and styles, and I think it is very beautiful when you begin to watch people open up the hemisphere of their minds to the creativity of the Holy Spirit.

That's why I believe the whole ministry of arts should be married to the ministry of the Prophet, since every form of the arts is to move into the prophetic mode. In Scripture where it says, "Saul his thousands and David his ten thousands," the dancers prophesied in dance at that particular time. David had only killed a lion and a bear. From the moment Saul heard the prophecy, he kept his eye on David.

We can see that the Prophets were very dramatic. In fact, the Prophets functioned as God's drama troop. They acted out and demonstrated their prophecies. This is true with many of the Prophets in the Old Testament.

In Jeremiah 27, God caused Jeremiah to move into a dramatic prophecy where He began to tell

Jeremiah:

> "... *Make thee bonds and yokes, and put them upon thy neck,*
>
> "*And send them to the king of Edom, and to the king of Moab, and to the king of the Ammonites, and to the king of Tyrus, and to the king of Zidon, by the hand of the messengers which come to Jerusalem unto Zedekiah king of Judah.*
>
> "*And command them to say unto their masters, Thus saith the Lord of hosts, the God of Israel; Thus shall ye say unto your masters;*
>
> "*I have made the earth, the man and the beast that are upon the ground, by my great power and by my outstretched arm, and have given it unto whom it seemed meet unto me.*"
>
> Jeremiah 27:2-5

As we read on, we can see that God used Jeremiah to dramatize the Word of the Lord that he was given at that particular time in the beginning of the reign of Jehoiakim, who was the son of Josiah, the king of Judah.

God caused another Prophet, Ezekiel, to become speechless and to begin to demonstrate the Word of the Lord.

> "*And the hand of the Lord was there upon me; and he said unto me, Arise, go forth into the plain, and I will there talk with thee.*
>
> "*Then I arose, and went forth into the plain: and, behold, the glory of the Lord stood there, as the glory which I saw by the river of Chebar: and*

I fell on my face.

"Then the Spirit entered into me, and set me upon my feet, and spake with me, and said unto me, Go, shut thyself within thine house.

"But thou, O son of man, behold, they shall put bands upon thee, and shall bind thee with them, and thou shalt not go out among them:

"And I will make thy tongue cleave to the roof of thy mouth, that thou shalt be dumb, and shalt not be to them a reprover: for they are a rebellious house.

"But when I speak with thee, I will open thy mouth, and thou shalt say unto them, Thus saith the Lord God; He that heareth, let him hear; and he that for beareth, let him forbear: for they are a rebellious house."

Ezekiel 3:22-27

In Ezekiel 5, the Prophet Ezekiel was directed by the Spirit to cut his hair and scatter a third of it to the wind, smite a third of it with a knife, and burn a third of it in the midst of the city. So here again, we see God's dramatic anointing working through the Prophet to convey a message to the people.

Another prophetic drama is given in Ezekiel 4:12-15.

"And thou shalt eat it as barley cakes, and thou shalt bake it with dung that cometh out of man, in their sight.

"And the Lord said, Even thus shall the children of Israel eat their defiled bread among the Gentiles, whither I will drive them.

> *"Then said I, Ah Lord God! behold, my soul hath not been polluted; for from my youth up even till now have I not eaten of that which dieth of itself, or is torn in pieces; neither came there abominable flesh into my mouth.*
>
> *"Then he said unto me, Lo, I have given thee cow's dung for man's dung, and thou shalt prepare thy bread therewith."*

This dramatization was to illustrate that Israel would eat of the bread of the Gentiles, which was defiled bread.

Prophets acted out much of the Word of the Lord for the primary purpose of communicating images that God wanted to indelibly print on the minds of the people.

God used drama through another Prophet, Hosea. God told Hosea to take an adulteress wife, to marry a harlot, in order to demonstrate the adultery that Israel had committed. Here we actually begin to see God, in a way, singing the blues because of what Israel has done, and how Israel had rebelled and become an unfaithful wife.

> *"Then said the Lord unto me, Go yet, love a woman beloved of her friend, yet an adulteress, according to the love of the Lord toward the children of Israel, who look to other gods, and love flagons of wine.*
>
> *"So I bought her to me for fifteen pieces of silver, and for an homer of barley, and an half homer of barley:*

> *"And I said unto her, Thou shalt abide for me many days; thou shalt not play the harlot, and thou shalt not be for another man: so will I also be for thee.*
>
> *"For the children of Israel shall abide many days without a king, and without a prince, and without a sacrifice, and without an image, and without an ephod, and without teraphim:*
>
> *"Afterward shall the children of Israel return, and seek the Lord their God, and David their king; and shall fear the Lord and his goodness in the latter days."*

Hosea 3:1-5

God had the prophet Hosea demonstrate Israel's unfaithfulness.

On several occasions, the prophets were God's drama troop. God used prophets to dramatize the Word of the Lord so that it would be communicated with great clarity.

I believe that at some point we will have a time in the School of Prophets only for those who function in the arts. We will teach how to take the artistic ability God has given them and cause it to flow in the prophetic mode, teaching them how to sing prophecy, dramatize, and demonstrate the Word of the Lord. If they have ability in poetry, we will teach them how to communicate prophecy in poetry.

I would love to see an individual given a Word by the Spirit, then have another person whom God has anointed sing the Word, communicating it in that mode. Then have another individual communicate that same Word in mime. And then have a drama team dramatize the same Word of the Lord unrehearsed by the Spirit of God. In this way, we will not only hear the Word of the Lord, but we will see it in demonstration.

Agabus did this with Paul. He moved into an area of drama when he took Paul's girdle and showed him bound. Every time Paul saw a girdle, he remembered the prophetic Word of the Lord as demonstrated through Agabus.

You can literally give an individual a Word from the Lord by using a pencil as an illustration. Something that simple will work. Then every time that person hears the word *pencil* or sees a pencil, instant recall will come to mind concerning the prophecy that was given with the illustration of a pencil. I believe God wants to restore this type of creativity back into the Church.

The spirit of prophecy was fluent in the company of Prophets which Samuel was orchestrating.

> *"And Saul sent messengers to take David: and when they saw the company of the prophets prophesying, and Samuel standing as appointed over them, the Spirit of God was upon the messengers of Saul, and they also prophesied.*
> *"And when it was told Saul, he sent other messengers, and they prophesied likewise, and Saul sent messengers again the third time, and they prophesied also.*

> *"Then went he also to Ramah, and came to a great well that is in Sechu: and he asked and said, Where are Samuel and David? And one said, Behold, they be at Naioth in Ramah.*
>
> *"And he went thither to Naioth in Ramah: and the Spirit of God was upon him also, and he went on, and prophesied, until he came to Naioth in Ramah.*
>
> *"And he stripped off his clothes also, and prophesied before Samuel in like manner, and lay down naked all that day and all that night. Wherefore they say, Is Saul also among the prophets?"*
>
> I Samuel 19:20-24

I believe Saul's nakedness symbolized the fact that he came out of his kingly attire, rather than the thought that he was nude. I believe he removed the garb he usually wore which set him apart as king.

Samuel was appointed over the people in these verses. He was judging, discerning, and grooming them. I believe he was possibly even saying to some, "You know, your word is a little bit too lengthy" or "Just hold that right there." Sometimes many of us start giving words that are long and drawn out. I believe we should just bring the concentrated orange juice, and let the Holy Spirit take care of the rest. With a long, drawn-out message, the people often miss the heart of it.

Sometimes we need to get right to the point of what God is saying, for it is not the length of the message that categorizes you as a major or minor Prophet. It is the content of the message or the impact.

In Bible School, they used to say, "Speak up to be heard, speak to be appreciated, but never let anyone be glad to see you finish." I'm sure many of us have experienced ministries where we were glad when they took their seat.

God wants His Word to flow. That's why as you are faithful in the little that God gives you, there will be a time when God will give you room to bring lengthy words, but that won't come overnight.

Saul was after David. David went to the School of the Prophets and found a haven of rest. It was almost like David was in a cave. I believe that it was at the School of the Prophets where David learned how to worship, because when you see them coming down out of the hill of God, you see them with a tabret, a flute, and a pipe. Music was a very important part of worship in the School of the Prophets.

Have you ever heard someone play something and hit an off note? The note wasn't a wrong note, but it came at the wrong time. Sometimes you can bring a word that is of God, but it is brought at the wrong time. It is off key. I believe as the prophets heard music, it kept them in a certain flow and in a certain timing. They understood timing, rhythm flow, and the purpose of harmony.

The Office of the Prophet

"And he gave some, apostles; and some, prophets; and some, evangelists; and some, pastors and teachers."

Ephesians 4:11

We need to note that Pastors and Teachers are used as one word. Every Pastor must be able to feed. There is a fine line between a shepherd and a feeder.

Jesus said to Peter, "Lovest thou me? Feed my sheep." When you begin to analyze this, you can see that Jesus referred to two different aspects: one as a feeder and another as a shepherd.

In the flock of God, you also have goats and dogs. You are able to feed them, but you can't shepherd them. As a Pastor, I am not the shepherd to some who become members of the Church of Brooklyn. I am just a feeder to some because they refuse to be sheep. If they refuse to be sheep, that means they are either a goat or the shepherd's dog. They will be blessed by your teaching ministry, yet they will say, "Don't shepherd me. Feed me, but do not shepherd me. I have my own agenda."

We need to understand the difference between the shepherding of the sheep and the feeding of the flock.

Ephesians 4:12 and 13 gives the purpose for the Prophet and those who are set in governmental offices of the church by the appointment of God.

> *"For the perfecting of the saints, for the work of the ministry, for the edifying of the body of Christ:*
> *"Till we all come in the unity of the faith, and of the knowledge of the Son of God, unto a perfect man, unto the measure of the stature of the fulness of Christ":*

The primary function of the Prophet in a church is for the equipping of the Saints. It is known as a "ministry gift" in many circles, and it is a foundation ministry of the church. Notice why he said this.

> *"That we henceforth be no more children, tossed to and fro, and carried about with every wind of doctrine, by the sleight of men, and cunning craftiness, whereby they lie in wait to deceive";*
> Verse 14

Children are tossed to and fro. In the desert, there is something known as tumbleweed which never takes root. To be truthful, there is a lot of tumbleweed in the church (people who never take root). You will always have winds of doctrine, but it is wrong when you are tossed to and fro by them.

You have people who go to a deliverance church and suddenly they hear that a healing move is taking place somewhere else. They will uproot and follow the healing move for a while. Then they separate again and follow a move that is emphasizing discipline. After a couple of weeks, they become discontent and leave to follow a miracle ministry. They are tossed to and fro. They are like children, never taking root, blown about by every wind of doctrine.

Verses 15 and 16 continue:

"But speaking the truth in love, may grow up into him in all things, which is the head, even Christ:
"From whom the whole body fitly joined together and compacted by that which every joint supplieth, according to the effectual working in the measure of every part, maketh increase of the body unto the edifying of itself in love."

We have a problem getting properly joined together. Every joint is to supply by connecting; yet we have individuals ruling churches who are not Pastors. They are exhorting, they think they are Evangelists, and they prophesy.

God is going to get His Body in joint. He is going to dislocate in order to relocate. When there is a dislocation, the relocation is very painful, because you have to break the bone and reset it.

I believe we are coming into a time where the party is over, because God is dislocating in order to relocate. He is doing a resetting in the Body, and He is saying, "My Body shall not be out of joint."

Chapter 2

THE PROPHETIC FLOW

We need to be alert to the fact that there is a divine flow to the prophetic ministry. A divine flow and a divine order to all things.

Divine Order

> *"Follow after charity, and desire spiritual gifts [the things of the Spirit] but rather that ye may prophesy."*
> — I Corinthians 14:1

There is a ministry of tongues and interpretation, a ministry of the Prophet, and also a releasing of the body to contribute.

> *"If any man speak in an unknown tongue, let it be by two, or at the most by three, and that by course; and let one interpret."*
> I Corinthians 14:27

Tongues and interpretation are not the same thing as prophecy. I have heard Pastors say that there is to be no more than three prophecies in a service. That is erroneous. We need to understand that he was saying, "Let them speak, two or at most three, and let one interpret." So it seems as though he set some guidelines for the ministry of tongues and interpretation. Then in verses 28 and 29, he says:

"But if there be no interpreter, let him keep silence in the church; and let him speak to himself, and to God.
"Let the prophets speak two or three, and let the other judge."

This seems to imply that there is a ministry of tongues and interpretation that can take place in the congregation. Then there is a ministry where the Prophets begin to speak to the congregation. When he says, "let the other judge," I believe that means the other Prophets or the other elder Prophets should judge the word rather than the Body judge it. I don't believe that the Body would have the ability to judge, because they are there to be led. So it means, "Let the elders that are flowing in that same realm (in that same vein), let them begin to discern and judge."

"If any thing be revealed to another that sitteth by, let the first hold his peace."
Verse 30

So we can see that if anything is revealed to any of the other Prophets who are sitting by, let the first hold his peace.

I believe this is an area where the Lord is going to bring us into maturity, especially in team ministry. I have had the privilege of ministering in team ministry and in a company of Prophets while I was traveling around the country. In nearly every service (we would have three meetings a day), we would have two or three Prophets speak in every setting. Now, because of this, we appointed a senior Prophet for that setting, and he would set the pace or say what was to be done. While one person was ministering, one of the other Prophets, that was in that team often quickened. The Prophets were sensitive to the Spirit and would stop and say, "Come and share that." The person who was asked to share brought another dimension of what was in the mind and purpose of God. This type of flow can only be developed out of a covenant relationship, developing a sensitivity to the Spirit, and teaching people how to flow together.

Oftentimes when moving together in presbytery, you can sense when someone else has something. You must tell your flesh to decrease so the Holy Spirit can increase and have the freedom to flow through whomever He wills.

I believe we are going to begin to see ministry coming to the Body where God is not going to speak through one man, but He is going to speak through a plurality of men in bringing forth the full purposes of God.

However, with a senior man in charge, we will see what we read in Samuel. Samuel stood over the Prophets as being appointed over them, orchestrating and keeping the order and the flow so they wouldn't thrust one another through and so there would be no conflict.

> *"For ye may all prophesy one by one, that all may learn, and all may be comforted.*
> *"And the spirits of the prophets are subject to the prophets.*
> *"For God is not the author of confusion, but of peace . . ."*
>
> Verses 31-33

We want you to note that the spirit of the Prophets is subject to the Prophets. I've been in meetings where someone would begin to prophesy and the person in authority said, "Just hold that prophecy. Hold that word right there, and let me finish my thought." After the person had finished his thought, he said, "Okay, now give us the Word of the Lord." This is not out of order. It is completely in the divine flow and order. There are other times when you might tell someone, "Just hold that word. I will speak to you after the service."

I like what one particular local fellowship did. The Minister said that when the Word of the Lord comes, they acknowledge the voice of the King by having everyone stand. The elders stand; then the rest of the congregation stands to acknowledge that it is the voice of the King. When they felt it wasn't God, the elders would remain sitting, which means the congregation knows to put that word on the shelf. I thought it was an excellent way to handle prophecy in the local church.

The New Song

Singing a new song unto the Lord flows in the prophetic realm. A new song is usually an unrehearsed series of inspired words put to song.

There is a song that can come from the church to the Lord, and then there can be a song from the Lord to the church. I believe we will see the songs of the Lord bursting forth as never before.

Psalm 149 talks about singing a new song unto the Lord and the results of it.

> *"Praise ye the Lord. Sing unto the Lord a new song, and his praise in the congregation of saints.*
> *"Let Israel rejoice in him that made him: let the children of Zion be joyful in their King.*
> *"Let them praise his name in the dance: let them sing praises unto him with the timbrel and harp.*
> *"For the Lord taketh pleasure in his people: he will beautify the meek with salvation.*
> *"Let the saints be joyful in glory: let them sing aloud upon their beds.*
> *"Let the high praises of God be in their mouth, and a two-edged sword in their hand;*
> *"To execute vengeance upon the heathen, and punishments upon the people;*
> *"To bind their kings with chains, and their*

nobles with fetters of iron;
    "To execute upon them the judgment writ-
ten: this honour have all his saints. Praise ye the
Lord."

If you don't sing, we don't encourage you to sing a song of the Lord, especially in services. Reserve that for those who are gifted in that area. On a few occasions where someone was getting ready to sing, I have said, "Just speak the song." You see, that's scriptural, too.

    "And be not drunk with wine, wherein is
excess; but be filled with the Spirit;
    "Speaking to yourselves in psalms and hymns
and spiritual songs, singing and making melody
in your heart to the Lord;"
                                    Ephesians 5:18-19

There is a praying in the Spirit and a singing in the Spirit. Therefore, I believe that which we sing in the Spirit can also be sung in our understanding. There is also a praying in the Spirit and a praying in our understanding.

    "What is it then? I will pray with the spirit,
and I will pray with the understanding also: I will
sing with the spirit, and I will sing with the
understanding also."
                                    I Corinthians 14:15

You can take a child who has been trained a certain way, but if he continues to listen to a certain type of music, the very beat or rhythm of that music can drum past his soul into his thinking and get into his spirit, causing the child to do things that are totally against what the parents taught him. It is almost like hypnotism. I believe the church has been hypnotized by some songs.

We need to understand that when a song book does not line up with the Word of God, it needs to be thrown out!

I think when we begin to look at some of our songs, especially songs that we have sung in a lot of the tradititonal black churches, we see some of those songs have come out of slavery and we have brought them over into our spiritual experience. I am sure you know some of the songs I am talking about. Simply remember, when the song does not line up with the Word, throw it out and begin to sing the Psalms.

I personally believe that we need to sing the Scriptures again, to sing the Word of the Lord, and to proclaim the defeat of the enemies of God on the earth in songs.

Colossians 3:16 and 17 says:

"Let the word of Christ dwell in you richly in all wisdom; teaching and admonishing one another in psalms and hymns and spiritual songs, singing with grace in your hearts to the Lord.
"And whatsoever ye do in word or deed, do all in the name of the Lord Jesus, giving thanks to God and the Father by him."

I believe a church becomes whatever it sings. This verse says "Teaching and admonishing one another." Whatever we sing are the things that become a part of our spirit. We need to begin to sing songs like, "A Mighty Fortress Is Our God," songs that are victorious and triumphant, songs that begin to display a church that is going to be a glorious church — not a weak church.

As we begin to go into aspects of teaching and admonishing one another in songs, I believe we need to see the spirit of the songwriter rise in the House of the Lord. We can begin to teach the congregation, not only by the doctrine of standing up and speaking, but also by singing the message of the Lord.

Anointed Music

In the Old Testament, we have evidence of the fact that the minstrel released the prophetic anointing.

In II Kings 3:15, Elisha called for the minstrel.

> *"But now bring me a minstrel. And it came to pass, when the minstrel played, that the hand of the Lord came upon him."*

It seemed as though the minstrel set the pace and the tone for the prophetic anointing to begin to arise. I have found that oftentimes when the musicians are playing, they tend to orchestrate the tone of a meeting. I have found without fail that when the music is off-key or out of tune, you get off-the-wall prophecy. Something seems to go out of flow. I have watched at times when music was playing in the background softly, there would be an anointing in the room, there would be a flow, and if something got out of the flow, you could hear it almost instantly.

Music is so important in the church, because the worship service can almost determine the degree of the impact of the service.

In I Samuel 10:5-10, music was connected with the spirit of prophecy. We also see that in the temple, music released the glory of God.

> *"After that thou shalt come to the hill of God, where is the garrison of the Philistines: and it shall come to pass, when thou art come thither to the city, that thou shalt meet a company of prophets coming down from the high place with a psaltery, and a tabret, and a pipe, and a harp, before them; and they shall prophesy:*
>
> *"And the Spirit of the Lord will come upon thee, and thou shalt prophesy with them, and shalt be turned into another man.*
>
> *"And let it be, when these signs are come unto thee, that thou do as occasion serve thee; for God is with thee.*
>
> *"And thou shalt go down before me to Gilgal; and, behold, I will come down unto thee, to offer burnt offerings, and to sacrifice sacrifices of peace offerings: seven days shalt thou tarry, till I come to thee, and shew thee what thou shalt do.*

"And it was so, that when he had turned his back to go from Samuel, God gave him another heart: and all those signs came to pass that day.

"And when they came thither to the hill, behold, a company of prophets met him; and the Spirit of God came upon him, and he prophesied among them."

Are you beginning to see the importance of developing worship leaders to be seers in the realm of music who begin to flow in the prophetic realm?

Styles of Delivery

We have briefly touched on styles of delivery in the prophetic ministry. To me, one of the most beautiful things is to hear people prophesy in poetry. We used to do it quite a bit in our local fellowship, especially when we were in New Jersey. The people would come forth with the Word of the Lord in rhyme and poetry, and it was such a beautiful flow of the Holy Spirit.

Then you have singing prophecy where people can sing the Word of the Lord or the prophetic word, then there is symbolic prophecy, where the person has a way of demonstrating the Word of the Lord.

I remember when a man began to prophesy over me in our local church. He grabbed me by my tie, pulled me, and said, "The Word of the Lord is going to come upon you in such a degree that when you begin to prophesy, you will teach as if you are reaching out for a man's tie and pulling him. As you begin to prophesy, it will grab men's lives and pull them into the purposes of God." (He never let go of my tie the entire time he was prophesying!)

This same man once grabbed a woman's tongue. (This is another example of symbolic prophecy.) He told the woman to stick out her tongue, which she did. Now, for this type of stuff, you must know what you are doing! You'd better know the voice of the Lord! He grabbed the woman's tongue and said, "This is the thing that has been bringing much pain and hurt to others, and this is the thing that has brought much pain and hurt to you."

Even though this was a prophetic word of warning from the Lord, this same woman, some two years later, wrote a book which caused a split in the church.

It is interesting to move in the prophetic flow using symbolism. We have had opportunity to move in it a little, though it hasn't been a strong emphasis in our ministry. I believe that as the prophetic office continues to grow, the Lord will do more and more of this, but I believe it is reserved unto those who are mature.

Chapter 3

THE FUNCTION OF THE PROPHETIC WORD

In discussing the function of the prophetic word, we will examine four primary areas: judging prophecy, the support of the Prophet, the school of the Prophets, and the uses of the prophetic ministry.

Judging Prophecy

All prophecy must be judged. Anything that goes unjudged is dangerous. There was a woman who challenged me and said, "No one can judge prophecy."

I responded, "The Scripture says, 'Let the prophets speak two or three, and let the others judge.' " She said, "I know that, *but* how can you judge a prophecy?"

1. We can judge the spirit in which the prophecy is given.

37

2. I believe anything that goes unjudged is dangerous.

In the early 1980's, a particular church I was in got the revelation that there was going to be an earthquake on February 28. Many of these people sold their possessions, left the city, and went up into the mountain to await the earthquake.

Since I was prophesying regularly then, and I didn't sense the spirit behind the prophecy was anything the Holy Spirit had spoken to me, I said, "I believe when something like this is about to happen, God will have a way of witnessing it to a company of Prophets and to elders within the city."

I mean, why would God bypass the Pastors of the church and speak something into the flock that the elders are not aware of?

When we look at order in the Kingdom of God, we need to understand that even the letters that were written to the seven churches were written to Pastors of the seven churches — not to a local Prophet in the flock. We need to understand order and authority. If we don't, we will miss the purposes of God.

Any word that is given should be confirmed, spoken, or witnessed to the elders. If it does not witness to the Elders, then you don't need to move on that word.

In the prediction of the earthquake, the people

came back a week after it was supposed to have occurred with egg on their faces, because the earthquake didn't take place.

We now have people selling their homes and doing all kinds of different things, because they say the coming of the Lord is going to be on a specific day. The whole thing sounds good, but the danger of building a doctrine on typology is that it doesn't hold any weight. It is sad to see what happens to the people caught up in these things when they don't occur as predicted.

Prophecy must bear witness in your spirit and in the spirit of the Prophets.

> *"This is the third time I am coming to you. **In the mouth of two or three witnesses shall every word be established."***
> II Corinthians 13:1

The way you can judge another individual's ministry is whether what he is speaking is coming to pass or not.

> *"When a prophet speaketh in the name of the Lord, if the thing follow not, nor come to pass, that is the thing which the Lord hath not spoken, but the prophet hath spoken it presumptuously: thou shalt not be afraid of him."*
> Deuteronomy 18:22

Another major way of judging prophecy is that *it must be in harmony with Scripture.* God will never speak anything that is contrary to His Word.

David said of God's Word, *"The words of the Lord are pure words: as silver tried in a furnace of earth, purified seven times"* (Psalm 12:6).

When we hear words that are spoken and we know they don't measure up with the principles of God's Word, we know it is a word we are not to receive.

"We have also a more sure word of prophecy; whereunto ye do well that ye take heed, as unto a light that shineth in a dark place, until the day dawn, and the day star arise in your hearts:

"Knowing this first, that no prophecy of the scripture is of any private interpretation.

"For the prophecy came not in old time by the will of man: but holy men of God spake as they were moved by the Holy Ghost."

II Peter 1:19-21

The Bible also says, *"For there are three that bear record in heaven, the Father, the Word, and the Holy Ghost: and these three are one"* (I John 5:7).

When the Spirit of God is speaking, He will not speak something that is out of harmony with the Father and the Word. The prophecy must be in harmony with Scripture, and every word that is spoken must be tried. It must be tried and examined to see whether it measures up with the Scriptures.

"As for God, his way is perfect: the word of the Lord is tried: he is a buckler to all those that trust in him."

Psalm 18:30

Support of the Prophet

I believe the reason why we haven't seen the restoration of the Prophet's office of the church is because we have a lot of Prophets who are functioning as Pastors. The church has not come to a revelation of how to properly support ministry.

As I shared with you earlier, I am not talking about an individual who stands up in the church to prophesy. I believe that Prophets in the church are to be according to Ephesians 4 and confirmed by the elders in the Body. That means they have been examined, proven, and hands have been laid on them for ordination and separation for that purpose.

I believe we are going to begin to see churches where not only is the Pastor functioning full-time, but we will see Apostles, Evangelists, and Prophets also functioning on a full-time basis. We are going to see the whole plurality of ministry working together toward the perfecting of the Body, functioning as elders and taking oversight of the flock of God.

It is interesting to note in the Old Testament that whenever someone went to see the Prophet, he did not go empty-handed. The people always took something to the Prophet.

I remember when I was growing up, my mother always taught us that whenever you went to someone's house, take something with you. We always took something, even if it was a couple of sodas, some juice, a cake, or a pie.

When you go to the doctor, you take something with you, whether it is your insurance card, your checkbook, or some cash. When you go to the accountant, you take something with you. When you go to the lawyer, you are going to take something with you. We are not talking about $5 or $10 either. I am sure all of you know that one consultation can easily cost $100.

How much more should we bring something with us when we go to the servants of the Most High God? Are you getting the picture?

If someone ministers unto you without holding back spiritual things, you should minister back to that person without holding back your carnal things. That's just a principle of the Kingdom of God that I think we need to implement in the Church.

We can take some examples from Saul.

"And the asses of Kish Saul's father were lost. And Kish said to Saul his son, Take now one of the servants with thee, and arise, go seek the asses.
"And he passed through mount Ephraim, and

passed through the land of Shalisha, but they found them not: then they passed through the land of Shalim, and there they were not: and he passed through the land of the Benjamites, but they found them not.

"And when they were come to the land of Zuph, Saul said to his servant that was with him, Come, and let us return; lest my father leave caring for the asses, and take thought for us.

"And he said unto him, Behold now, there is in this city a man of God, and he is an honourable man; all that he saith cometh surely to pass: now let us go thither; peradventure he can shew us our way that we should go.

"Then said Saul to his servant, But, behold, if we go, what shall we bring the man? for the bread is spent in our vessels, and there is not a present to bring to the man of God: what have we?

"And the servant answered Saul again, and said, Behold, I have here at hand the fourth part of a shekel of silver: that will I give to the man of God, to tell us our way."

I Samuel 9:3-8

It was their custom to take something to the man of God, and it seemed as though Israel honored the men of God that were in their nation.

It is a custom of the Jews to esteem the Rabbi very highly and to see that he is well taken care of. They feel that the highest thing one could ever be is a teacher of the law. They recognize that a natural teacher is teaching only things for this life, while a spiritual teacher is teaching things for this life and the life to come.

Naaman took a gift to the Prophet of God, although his gift was refused by the Prophet.

> *"Then went he (Naaman) down, and dipped himself seven times in Jordan, according to the saying of the man of God: and his flesh came again like unto the flesh of a little child, and he was clean.*
>
> *"And he returned to the man of God, he and all his company, and came, and stood before him: and he said, Behold, now I know that there is no God in all the earth, but in Israel: now therefore, I pray thee, take a blessing of thy servant.*
>
> *"But he said, As the Lord liveth, before whom I stand, I will receive none. And he urged him to take it; but he refused."*
>
> II Kings 5:14-16

Naaman didn't bring a pair of old, worn-out shoes or the smallest bill he could find to offer the Prophet. He brought several things to present to the Prophet, although Elisha refused them.

We see another example of presents being brought for the Prophet of God in II Kings 8:7-9:

> *"And Elisha came to Damascus, and Ben-hadad the king of Syria was sick; and it was told him, saying, The man of God is come hither.*
>
> *"And the king said unto Hazael, Take a present in thine hand, and go, meet the man of God, and enquire of the Lord by him, saying, Shall I recover of this disease?*

"So Hazael went to meet him, and took a present with him, even of every good thing of Damascus, forty camels' burden, and came and stood before him, and said, Thy son Ben-hadad king of Syria hath sent me to thee, saying, Shall I recover of this disease?"

These people wouldn't think of going to a man of God without an offering, and they certainly weren't cheap in their giving.

Even when the Queen of Sheba visited Solomon, she brought gifts to him.

"And she gave the king an hundred and twenty talents of gold, and of spices very great store, and precious stones: there came no more such abundance of spices as these which the queen of Sheba gave to king Solomon."

I Kings 10:10

I can't wait until those days come and someone says, "Prophet Jordan, I must come and see you," and he appears loaded with gifts to bless the work of the Lord.

School of the Prophets

In I Samuel 19:18-24, as we previously discussed, Samuel was the head of a School of the Prophets.

Elisha also became the head of the School of the Prophets in the transference of spirits that occurred when he received Elijah's mantle. Before he could receive Elijah's mantle, however, I believe that in the School of the Prophets, Elisha looked at Elijah as a father. (You cannot receive the spirit of an individual unless you are willing to be fathered or nurtured by that person.) This relationship is like a teacher and a student where the student is being discipled.

A company (or school) of prophets is referred to in Samuel's conversation with Saul, whom he had just anointed. These were Samuel's words to Saul:

> *"After that thou shalt come to the hill of God, where is the garrison of the Philistines: and it shall come to pass, when thou art come thither to the city, that thou shalt meet a company of prophets coming down from the high place with a psaltery, and a tabret, and a pipe, and a harp, before them, and they shall prophesy:*
>
> *"And the Spirit of the Lord will come upon thee, and thou shalt prophesy with them, and shalt be turned into another man.*
>
> *"And let it be, when these signs are come unto thee, that thou do as occasion serve thee; for God is with thee."*
>
> I Samuel 10:5-7

Uses of the Prophetic Ministry

The three primary purposes or uses of the prophetic ministry are to point in direction, to confirm, and to bring correction and building.

In verse 8 of I Samuel 10, Samuel was still speaking to Saul when he said:

"And thou shalt go down before me to Gilgal; and, behold, I will come down unto thee, to offer burnt offerings, and to sacrifice sacrifices of peace offerings: seven days shalt thou tarry, till I come to thee, and shew thee what thou shalt do."

In Acts 13:1 and 2, the Prophets and Teachers were together. As they fasted and ministered to the Lord, divine direction came to Barnabas and Saul.

"Now there were in the church that was at Antioch certain prophets and teachers; as Barnabas, and Simeon that was called Niger, and Lucius of Cyrene, and Manaen, which had been brought up with Herod the tetrarch, and Saul.

"As they ministered to the Lord, and fasted, the Holy Ghost said, Separate me Barnabas and Saul for the work whereunto I have called them."

I believe God wants to set us apart and cause us to move into His purpose.

In most New Testament ministry, we noted that men moved in apostolic team ministry. In other words, what we mean by apostolic team ministry is, they did not move in a one-man show, but it was a plurality of men ministering together under the unction and the anointing of the Holy Spirit.

In Acts 13, we see a separation by the Holy Spirit for team ministry.

"Now there were in the church that was at Antioch certain prophets and teachers; as Barnabas, and Simeon that was called Niger, and Lucius of Cyrene, and Manaen, which had been brought up with Herod the tetrarch, and Saul.

"As they ministered to the Lord, and fasted, the Holy Ghost said, Separate me Barnabas and Saul for the work whereunto I have called them.

"And when they had fasted and prayed, and laid their hands on them, they sent them away."

Acts 13:1-3

According to these verses, the early church moved in apostolic team ministry. Barnabas and Paul were sent out together. We know that Paul was an Apostle, and we are led to believe that Barnabas was a Prophet in the early church.

"And Joses, who by the apostles was surnamed Barnabas (which is, being interpreted, The son of consolation), a Levite, and of the country of Cyprus."

Acts 4:36

Barnabas' name actually meant "son of consolation" or "son of prophecy," so we are led to believe that he was a Prophet.

Paul and Barnabas went out together as Apostle and Prophet, ministering together in establishing the local church.

When there appeared to be some contention in the local church, Silas, another Prophet, came on the scene.

> *"And Paul chose Silas, and departed, being recommended by the brethren unto the grace of God.*
> *"And he went through Syria and Cilicia, confirming the churches."*
>
> Acts 15:40-41

In Acts 15:32, it says:

> *"And Judas and Silas, being prophets also themselves, exhorted the brethren with many words, and confirmed them."*

Paul, an apostle, took Barnabas, a Prophet, with him in ministry. Paul obviously recognized the value of a companion ministry. The Apostle and Prophet functioned and moved together in confirming and strengthening the churches.

> *"And he went through Syria and Cilicia, confirming the churches [or strengthening the churches.]"*
>
> Acts 15:41

We can see the importance of the team functioning together in ministry.

Another function of the prophet's ministry is to correct and to build. We see this clearly identified as the Word of the Lord came unto Jeremiah.

> *"Then the Lord put forth his hand, and touched*

*my mouth. And the Lord said unto me, Behold, I
have put my words in thy mouth.*

*"See, I have this day set thee over the nations
and over the kingdoms, to root out, and to pull
down, and to destroy, and to throw down, to build,
and to plant."*

Jeremiah 1:9-10

The church today that accepts the Prophet who
roots out, pulls and throws down, builds and
plants, will flourish and abound.

Chapter 4

MINISTRY OF TONGUES

Tongues and Interpretation

Tongues is a priestly ministry. I Corinthians 14:2 says:

> *"For he that speaketh in an unknown tongue speaketh not unto men, but unto God: for no man understandeth him; howbeit in the spirit he speaketh mysteries."*

There is no such thing as a message in tongues. When we speak in tongues, we are speaking to God. It seems as though when there is an utterance in tongues, it is not so much a message being given to the congregation as it is communing or a priestly ministry of that individual unto the Father. The Bible says when you speak in an unknown tongue, you are speaking unto God.

51

Some of our brethren have taught that there is a prayer language that is to be used in private devotions which differs from the gift of tongues. The gift of tongues for the church would be that there's a message coming to the church, but this doesn't seem to be in harmony with the Scripture. The Bible says that when we speak in tongues we are speaking unto God, not unto men.

I believe that when we hear the interpretation of tongues, we are going to begin to hear the interpretation of what the individual has been speaking unto God. It can be praise or prayer or prayer on behalf of the congregation. It can be speaking of the greatness of God. The only thing I can liken it to in the Old Testament is David's Psalms unto the Lord. Speaking in tongues is connected with singing in the Spirit.

I Corinthians 14:2-4 in the Amplified Bible says:

"For one who speaks in an [unknown] tongue speaks not to men but to God, for no one understands or catches his meaning, because in the (Holy) Spirit he utters secrets, truths and hidden things [not obvious to the understanding].

"But [on the other hand], the one who prophesies — who interprets the divine will and purpose in inspired preaching and teaching — speaks to men for their upbuilding and constructive spiritual progress and encouragement and consolation.

"He who speaks in a [strange] tongue edifies and improves himself, but he who prophesies —

interpreting the divine will and purpose and teaching with inspiration — edifies and improves the church and promotes growth [in Christian wisdom, piety, holiness and happiness].

J.B. Phillips translates verse 2 as follows:

The man who speaks in a "tongue" addresses not men (for no one understands a word he says) but God: and only in his spirit is he speaking spiritual secrets.

Tongues is a ministry of prayer and praise. I Corinthians 14:14 says, *"For if I pray in an unknown tongue, my spirit prayeth, but my understanding is unfruitful."* So when I am speaking in tongues, my spirit is praying.

Paul continues:

"What is it then? I will pray with the spirit, and I will pray with the understanding also..."
                                                     Verse 15

Speaking in tongues is a language that is God given by the Holy Spirit, and we are speaking unto God. Paul said:

"Even so ye, forasmuch as ye are zealous of spiritual gifts, seek that ye may excel to the edifying of the church.
"Wherefore let him that speaketh in an unknown tongue pray that he may interpret.
"Yet in the church I had rather speak five words

with my understanding, that by my voice I might teach others also, than ten thousand words in an unknown tongue."

I Corinthians 14:12-13, 19

Now we know that tongues are to be interpreted when used in public assembly. We need to differentiate that tongues are interpreted, not translated.

In our local fellowship, sometimes an utterance in tongues will come forth and the interpretation might be, "I will bless the Lord with all of my heart, and I will exalt Him for His Name is great. He alone is worthy to be praised." In this situation, the interpretation is what the individual's spirit is saying unto God.

Praying With the Spirit

As we mentioned previously, when you pray in the spirit, you are speaking mysteries unto God, and you are also building (or charging) yourself up:

"He that speaketh in an unknown tongue edifieth himself; but he that prophesieth edifieth the church."

I Corinthians 14:4

"But ye, beloved, building up yourselves on your most holy faith, praying in the Holy Ghost,'

Jude 20

Praying in the Spirit will also bring a refreshing. Isaiah proclaims:

"For precept must be upon precept, precept upon precept; line upon line, line upon line; here a little, and there a little:

"For with stammering lips and another tongue will he speak to this people.

"To whom he said, This is the rest wherewith ye may cause the weary to rest; and this is the refreshing: yet they would not hear."

Isaiah 28:10-12

A parallel verse is found in I Corinthians 14:21.

Praying in the spirit will produce revelation. While speaking in tongues, you are speaking divinely granted secrets or mysteries. I believe that as you begin to pray those mysteries, you will begin to pray with the understanding. God will cause you to tap into or get a glimpse of some of the things He wants to be revealed to you or purposes He wants to explode on the inside of you.

Diversities of Tongues

"And God hath set some in the church, first apostles, secondarily prophets, thirdly teachers, after that miracles, then gifts of healings, helps, governments, diversities of tongues."

I Corinthians 12:28

For years I thought that the diversities of tongues were possibly different dialects. It can possibly mean that, but I want to submit something else to you. In Ephesians 6:18-19, Paul says:

> *"Praying always with all prayer and supplica-*
> *tion in the Spirit, and watching thereunto with all*
> *perseverance and supplication for all saints;*
> *"And for me, that utterance may be given unto*
> *me, that I may open my mouth boldly, to make*
> *known the mystery of the gospel,"*

I believe there can also be different types of prayers that can be prayed. In Acts 2:11, when they heard of speaking in tongues, they heard them "speaking the wonderful works of God":

> *"Cretes and Arabians, we do hear them speak*
> *in our tongues the wonderful works of God."*

It seems to imply that when they were speaking in tongues, they were *praising God*. They were addressing God. They were speaking the wonderful works of God.

Diversities of tongues are also for intercession.

Romans 8:26-27 mentions:

> *"Likewise the Spirit also helpeth our infirmi-*
> *ties: for we know not what we should pray for as*
> *we ought: but the Spirit itself maketh intercession*
> *for us with groanings which cannot be uttered.*
> *"And he that searcheth the hearts knoweth*
> *what is the mind of the Spirit, because he maketh*
> *intercession for the saints according to the will of*
> *God."*

There have been times when my wife and I have

ministered and I felt a real prompting to speak in tongues. When I got ready to interpret, I was interpreting a Psalm or something that was in my spirit or sometimes the Spirit was making intercession for the congregation for something they were going through at the time. Then the interpretation began to come in the form of a prayer. The Holy Spirit prompted intercession for a particular Body.

Often when I would hear people speaking in tongues, I could actually hear weeping in their hearts. I could hear people praying for their family, and I knew that the interpretation of the tongues was something for them personally.

I'll give you another example. A friend of mine, a Spanish brother, was praying. We were sitting on the same row in a church. A woman behind him started speaking in tongues. Suddenly, she started speaking perfect Spanish. He turned around and looked at her as she was praying. He understood every word she said in perfect Spanish. She was saying, "Lord, that battle. Let it be. Let it be. Let the battle be. Let the battle be." That's all she kept saying.

So it makes you begin to conclude the tongues and interpretation that we've been hearing is just the speaking unto God. Also, when there is a speaking in tongues, there can be the blessing with the Spirit. This is presented in I Corinthians 14:16:

> *"Else when thou shalt bless with the spirit, how shall he that occupieth the room of the un-*

learned say Amen at thy giving of thanks, seeing he understandeth not what thou sayest?"

Paul never, in any of these cases, seems to imply that there's a message coming, but when there is an utterance in tongues, there can be the blessing with the Spirit. You were giving thanks. You did a good job at giving thanks, but the others were not edified. They couldn't say Amen, and agree with your thanks, because they did not know what you were saying. It seems to imply that whenever tongues were spoken in the Scripture, there was something that was addressed to God rather than to men.

Baptism of the Spirit

The 120 in the upper room on the day of Pentecost received the baptism of the Holy Spirit and began to speak in other tongues. Let's review Acts 2:1-4:

"And when the day of Pentecost was fully come, they were all with one accord in one place.
"And suddenly there came a sound from heaven as of a rushing mighty wind, and it filled all the house where they were sitting.
"And there appeared unto them cloven tongues like as of fire, and it sat upon each of them.
"And they were all filled with the Holy Ghost, and began to speak with other tongues, as the Spirit gave them utterance."

In Acts 8, we see that the people of Samaria received the baptism of the Holy Spirit and spoke in tongues.

> "But when they [the people of Samaria] believed Philip preaching the things concerning the Kingdom of God, and the name of Jesus Christ, they were baptized, both men and women.
>
> "Then Simon himself believed also: and when he was baptized, he continued with Philip, and wondered, beholding the miracles and signs which were done.
>
> "Now when the Apostles which were at Jerusalem heard that Samaria had received the word of God, they sent unto them Peter and John:
>
> "Who, when they were come down, prayed for them, that they might receive the Holy Ghost:
>
> "(For as yet he was fallen upon none of them: only they were baptized in the name of the Lord Jesus.)
>
> "Then laid they their hands on them, and they received the Holy Ghost."
>
> Acts 8:12-17

Certain disciples were baptized after John's baptism. I call this the "law of realization." They were saved, but they hadn't come into the truth of the baptism of the Spirit, so they did not walk in it. You can only walk in whatever you hear or whatever you have been taught.

> "And it came to pass, that, while Apollos was at Corinth, Paul having passed through the upper coasts came to Ephesus: and finding certain disciples,
>
> "He said unto them, Have ye received the Holy

Ghost since ye believed? And they said unto him, We have not so much as heard whether there be any Holy Ghost.

"And he said unto them, Unto what then were ye baptized? And they said, Unto John's baptism.

"Then said Paul, John verily baptized with the baptism of repentance, saying unto the people, that they should believe on him which should come after him, that is, on Christ Jesus.

"When they heard this, they were baptized in the name of the Lord Jesus.

"And when Paul had laid his hands upon them, the Holy Ghost came on them; and they spake with tongues and prophesied."

Acts 19:1-6

Cornelius' household received the baptism of the Holy Spirit as Peter preached Christ unto them. Acts 10:44-48 gives the account:

"While Peter yet spake these words, the Holy Ghost fell on all them which heard the Word.

"And they of the circumcision which believed were astonished, as many as came with Peter, because that on the Gentiles also was poured out the gift of the Holy Ghost.

"For they heard them speak with tongues, and magnify God. Then answered Peter,

"Can any man forbid water, that these should not be baptized, which have received the Holy Ghost as well as we?

"And he commanded them to be baptized in the name of the Lord. Then prayed they him to tarry certain days."

Chapter 5

THE OFFICE OF THE PROPHET

The office of the Prophet is ordained of God as indicated in Ephesians 4:11. In this chapter, we will address the topics of Old Testament Prophets, New Testament Prophets and women who stood in the office of Prophetess.

Old Testament Prophets

The first mention of the office of the Prophet in the Old Testament concerns Abraham in Genesis 20:7. *"Now therefore restore the man his wife, for he is a prophet. . ."*

The first time we began to hear of Abram and the word *Prophet*, it was connected with prayer, so every Prophet must have a prayer life. He must have an open channel with the Lord. If his channel is not open between himself and the Lord, he will not hear with clarity the things he needs to hear.

There were Prophets in Scripture that led the children of Israel. These Prophets were Moses, Samuel, Elijah and Elisha. A Prophet is a supportive ministry, but a Prophet can also be a leader in the church.

Then we have several writing Prophets in the Old Testament, both major and minor prophets.

New Testament Prophets

In the New Testament, there were Prophets of confirmation (Acts 15:41), Prophets of exhortation (Acts 15:32), and Prophets who foretold.

We see an example of foretelling when Agabus saw in the Spirit that Paul would be bound by the Jews at Jerusalem.

> *"And as we tarried there many days, there came down from Judaea, a certain prophet, named Agabus.*
> *"And when he was come unto us, he took Paul's girdle, and bound his own hands and feet, and said, Thus saith the Holy Ghost, So shall the Jews at Jerusalem bind the man that owneth this girdle, and shall deliver him into the hands of the Gentiles."*
>
> Acts 21:10-11

When I was interviewed on TBN (Trinity Broadcasting Network), the interviewer asked, "What is the difference between prophecy and fortune-telling?" I felt that was an excellent question, because people have attended church meetings conducted like *charismatic fortune-telling.*

Some of the primary differences are:

1. A Prophet is motivated only by the Holy Spirit.

2. Whatever they do, it must bring glory and honor to Jesus. They must point people toward the Lord, not toward anything other than the Lordship of Jesus Christ.

3. A New Testament Prophet is not so much one who foretells, as much as he communicates the purpose of God to the individual.

Obviously in the purpose of God, there may be some telling of some things that will come beforehand, but that's not the main thing. I found that God wants to deal with His purpose in your life, where you are presently and how far off you are from its fulfillment.

Other Names for Prophets

Old Testament Prophets were known as *seers.* You can be a seer in the realm of music. David was a seer in this respect. I believe that within the local church, God places individuals in certain functions to be seers or guards in these realms.

I believe an individual who is in the music department to oversee the music in the house should become a seer. This person should ask,

"What God wants to communicate to this Body?"

Just because an individual is a seer in the house doesn't necessarily mean he will come into the position as a Prophet or an Elder. But I believe the Father wants to bring many of us into areas where we are able to see His purposes in which we are to function in and carry out those functions, especially if we are leading certain areas of the Body of Christ.

I also believe God will raise up different individuals to become seers for certain leaders. I believe there will be certain individuals God will place in my life to become eyes (a seer) for me.

Another name for Prophet was *man of God.*

> "*And the king said unto Hazael, Take a present in thine hand and go, meet the **man of God**, and enquire of the Lord by him, saying, Shall I recover of this disease?*"
>
> II Kings 8:8

Another name for Prophet was *Watchman on the wall.* Ezekiel was called "a watchman unto the house of Israel."

> "*Son of man, I have made thee a watchman unto the house of Israel: therefore hear the word at my mouth, and give them warning from me.*"
>
> Ezekiel 3:17

A parallel verse is found in Ezekiel 33:7 concerning Ezekiel's position as "a watchman unto the house of Israel."

Another name for Prophet is *Prophetess*, the name given a female Prophet.

Female Prophets

Although there is still controversy in some circles about women in church leadership roles as Bishops and Elders, we are given several examples of female Prophets in Scripture. God placed certain women in the role of Prophetess in Scripture.

Miriam is one example of a Prophetess.

> *"And Miriam the Prophetess, the sister of Aaron, took a timbrel in her hand; and all the women went out after her with timbrels and with dances.*
> *"And Miriam answered them, Sing ye to the Lord, for he hath triumphed gloriously; the horse and his rider hath he thrown into the sea."*
>
> Exodus 15:20-21

Deborah was a Prophetess.

> *"And Deborah, a Prophetess, the wife of Lapidoth, she judged Israel at that time.*
> *"And she dwelt under the palm tree of Deborah between Ramah and Beth-el in mount Ephraim: and the children of Israel came up to her for judgment."*
>
> Judges 4:4-5

Huldah is another Old Testament Prophetess.

> *"So Hilkiah the priest, and Ahikam, and Ach-*
> *bor, and Shaphan, and Asahiah, went unto*
> *Huldah the Prophetess, the wife of Shallum the*
> *son of Tikvah, the son of Harhas, keeper of the*
> *wardrobe; (now she dwelt in Jerusalem in college);*
> *and they communed with her."*
>
> II Kings 22:14

A parallel verse indicating that Huldah was a Prophetess is found in II Chronicles 34:22.

Isaiah's wife was a Prophetess.

> *"Moreover the Lord said unto me, Take thee a*
> *great roll, and write in it with a man's pen con-*
> *cerning Maher-shalal-hash-baz.*
> *"And I took unto me faithful witnesses to*
> *record, Uriah the priest, and Zechariah the son of*
> *Jeberechiah.*
> *"And I went unto the Prophetess; and she*
> *conceived, and bare a son. Then said the Lord to*
> *me, Call his name Maher-shalal-hash-baz.*
> *"For before the child shall have knowledge to*
> *cry, My father, and my mother, the riches of Da-*
> *mascus and the spoil of Samaria shall be taken*
> *away from the king of Assyria."*
>
> Isaiah 8:1-4

Anna was a New Testament Prophetess.

> *"And there was one Anna, a Prophetess, the*
> *daughter of Phanuel, of the tribe of Aser: she was*

of a great age, and had lived with an husband seven years from her virginity;

"And she was a widow of about fourscore and four years, which departed not from the temple, but served God with fastings and prayers night and day.

"And she coming in that instant gave thanks likewise unto the Lord, and spake of him to all them that looked for redemption in Jerusalem."

Luke 2:36-38

The role of the Prophet (or Prophetess) must be accepted and respected today so that every member of the Body of Christ finds his (or her) place, that every joint in the Body will be in place. The rooting out, the pulling down, the destroying, the throwing down, the building and the planting of the Prophet must take place for the entire Body of Christ to be perfected and in position to take up residence in their proper country — the New Jerusalem.

Amen and Amen!

BIOGRAPHICAL SKETCH

DR. E. BERNARD JORDAN

DR. E. BERNARD JORDAN is the founder and pastor of Zoe Ministries/The Church of Brooklyn, which meets in Manhattan at 310 Riverside Drive. The central office is located in Brooklyn, New York.

He is the husband of Debra, who functions as a Prophetess alongside her husband, and together they are the proud parents of five children: Naomi, Bethany, Joshua, Aaron and Yakim Manasseh.

Under the guidance of the Holy Spirit, he has a strong revelatory teaching ministry concerning the Gospel in relation to present-day truth and the releasing of the Body of Christ in the manifestations of the Holy Spirit.

Primarily, Dr. Jordan is noted for his prophetic ministry, giving forth the Word of the Lord to thousands of people from all walks of life; such as businessmen, government leaders, ambassadors and royalty. He has also been used to impact many churches with the Word of the Lord both nationally and internationally. He has travelled extensively throughout the United States, the Caribbean, Germany, Korea, and South Africa. In Swaziland, he was used to minister to the Queen and the Royal Family, and brought the nation into a new awareness of intercessory prayer.

In 1988, his ministry was highlighted by an invitation to minister at the United Nations to a special assembly of ambassadors and diplomats concerning South Africa. In February 1992, he was again summoned to the United Nations to bring the Word of the Lord.

In 1990, Dr. Jordan addressed a group of Korean students at the United Nations, and travelled to Korea to speak at a major prayer conference in that nation.

He has authored and published 18 books, with many more awaiting their unveiling. He has also founded THE SCHOOL OF THE PROPHETS, a ministerial training school that teaches scriptural principles for those who desire to serve in Christian ministry.

Dr. Jordan also conducts "The Law of Opulence," a motivational seminar designed to teach the principles of prosperity to God's people. He is the recipient of numerous awards, titles and honors for the work which he has accomplished in the Kingdom of God. He is a man whose heart burns with the call of destiny and the determination to fulfill God's will.

VIDEO CASSETTES
BY BISHOP E. BERNARD JORDAN

RACIAL ETHICS OF THE KINGDOM

Confronts the intrinsic racism that has permeated Christian doctrine. A Thorough study of the "traditional" teachings of the Church unveils a deliberate strain of racism that fosters white supremacy and eradicates the image of God within the African-American. It was this same strain of religiosity that soothed the consciousness of many and justified the atrocities of slavery in America. This series delineates the patent effects of such doctrine and restores the dignity of all races under God that were created for His divine purpose. 4-Video series $80

FREEDOM: THE WAY OF LIBERATION

A clarification of God's true definition of freedom and the resulting implications of the facade of liberty that continues to enslave the African-American community. The continuous assault of malevolent imagery that society uses to deliberately cripple the function of an entire race of people and deface their cultural legacy actually recreates Jesus Christ, the anointed Deliver of men, into an effigy that is crucified afresh on a daily basis. True freedom will emerge as the traditions of men are dethroned and replaced by the uncompromising Word of God that will cut every insidious lie asunder. This series will offend many who have been blinded by the hypnotic lies that have lulled their purpose to sleep, and challenge others to look beyond the veil of mediocrity and prejudice and behold the beauty of God's original intention towards men. This four-tape series is an unforgettable encounter with past, present and future as it proclaims the manifest destiny of the African-American and the Kingdom of God. 4-Video series $80

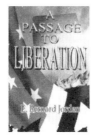

A PASSAGE TO LIBERATION

"A Passage to Liberation" is a thought-provoking edict against the dichotomy of society's offer of "Liberation" towards the African-American, versus their true liberty as ordained by God. The ingrained levels of prejudice that are encountered on a daily basis are indicated through the ethical teachings of the Word of God. Your spirit will be stirred to defy the implied boundaries of racial denigration, and thrust into the zenith of your capabilities through Jesus Christ. 4-Video series $80

PREPARATION FOR LEADERSHIP

A scathing indictment upon the insidious racism that permeates American society. Using Exodus Chapter 2 as his premise, Bishop Jordan delivers a powerful comparison between the pattern of oppressive leadership that requires divine intervention in the affairs of men and culminated in the appointment of Moses as the deliverer of Israel with the oppressive leadership that the African-American encounters within society and within the walls of the Church. Frightening in its accuracy, this teaching, though disturbing to the ear, is truly the Word of the Lord for this hour, for there are serious ramifications that the Church must contend with if she is to bring a solution to the crisis of woe in this nation.
4-Video series $80

THE SPIRIT OF THE OPPRESSOR

This series, The Spirit of the Oppressor, by Bishop E. Bernard Jordan, attacks the very fiber of societal influence that manipulates the gospel to justify racial supremacy. The insidious attitudes that permeate the Church are also addressed, for judgment begins in the House of God. By understanding that the Church is called to be the example for the world to follow, this series is powerful in its ability to expose the evil that lurks in the shadows of the "acceptable norm," and echoes a clarion call for deliverance from the lie that masquerades as the truth. Are you REALLY ready for the Word of the Lord?

4-Video series .... $80 also available as a book.

NO MORE HANDOUTS

In this series, Bishop E. Bernard Jordan addresses an inflammatory issue that has been instilled as a mindset within an entire nation of people. The American society has methodically caused generations of African-Americans to become dependent to a system that keeps them in a cycle of expectation that the government will always be their source of blessing. Bishop Jordan delineates the intention of God to bring prosperity to His people, thus charging them to turn their attention from the governmental system and discover the treasure that God has placed in their hands, for God is to be their source! This series is challenging and will force you to use your God-given abilities to thing creatively and generate wealth. You don't need anyone's permission to increase, for God has already decreed that you would multiply and wax exceedingly mighty!! This radical message is for a radical people!!

4-Video series $80

THE CROSSING

Bishop E. Bernard Jordan delivers a powerful teaching that defines the attitude that one must take as they begin to cross over their Jordan into the promised land. The paradigms of the old must be shattered as the image of change comes into view. One cannot embrace a new day loaded with old apparatus that is inoperative; old concepts that only brought you to a place of desperation and frustration. Rather, one must search the Word of God and renew your mind to Kingdom thinking that will bring elevation into your life. This series will sweep the cobwebs of mediocrity out of your life, and provoke you to a higher plane of right thinking that will thrust you into the path of dreams fulfilled. Straightforward in his approach, Bishop Jordan preaches a message that is inflammatory to the lies that have taken residence in your mind, and instills the purity of truth that is the nature of Almighty God. 4-Video series $80

UNDRESSING THE LIE

In this series, Bishop E. Bernard Jordan addresses a crucial issue in the Body of Christ -- RACISM. This series will captivate those who are true lovers of truth, for Jesus Christ is the Truth, and many have hidden Him and His cultural reality from the eyes of many. By conducting a thorough search of the Scriptures, Bishop Jordan identifies the Bible's description of Jesus that has been marred by the lies of those who wished to destroy an entire nation's concept of themselves, instead rendering theology that warped the image of God and denigrated them by teaching that they were cursed. Questions that have wandering in the minds of many for hundreds of years are answered as Bishop Jordan takes a strong stand to unmask the lies that have been masquerading as Truth. 4-Video series $80

LEGACY

In this series, Bishop E. Bernard Jordan expounds upon the African presence within the Scriptures. Combatting the misnomers that Africans were cursed by God and that they had very little to do with the unfolding of Biblical events, Bishop Jordan smashes the veil of delusion to cause the obvious truth to surface. During this season, God is causing a cultural renaissance to emerge. The oppressor of American society has lulled the minds of most people into a stupor of ignorance leaving them landless, powerless, and, once again, easy to enslave. The historical accounts within the Scriptures have been bequeathed as a legacy from our ancestors to proclaim the Word of the Lord against the sophisticated genocide that is affecting the African-American. A nation that ignores its past is doomed to repeat its failures in the future. Bishop Jordan brings clarity and balance to an inflammatory topic that is frequently misunderstood. 4-Video series $80

ECONOMICS: THE PATH TO EMPOWERMENT

This vital tape series by Bishop E. Bernard Jordan and Prophet Robert Brown deals with God's answers to the financial instability that has crippled the strength of the African-American nation. By defining the true motivation behind the onslaught of racism, Bishop Jordan and Prophet Brown give clear answers to the persistent societal obstacles that prevent most people from obtaining the true manifestation of God's intention for prosperity in their lives. The articulate questions that proceed from the heart of the nation shall be answered through the accumulation of wealth, for money shall answer all things. This teaching will expose the subtle racism that affects your financial future, and will provoke you into a mindset that will see obstacles as opportunities so that the full potential of God within you may express in your success! 2-Video series $40

NO LIBERATION WITHOUT VIOLENCE

This series will cause one to Scripturally discern the validity of the message of liberation that echoed through America during the 60's through Dr. Martin Luther King and Malcolm X. By holding their messages up to the scrutiny of the Word of God, one cannot help but conclude whose message was more palatable to society, versus the message that stood in the integrity of the Scripture. Challenging in its content, this series is designed to attack the shackles of passivity and charge you to recognize the brutal realities of today's society. You are called to understand the true liberty of the gospel that Jesus preached. 4-Video series $80

A NEW GENERATION

Bishop E. Bernard Jordan is at his best in this series which portrays the change in one's attitude that must take place in order to attain your maximum potential in God and proceed to your Canaan Land! Like Joshua, one must be ready to be strong and of a good courage as you confront racism in this day. This is a radical message to eradicate error and bring forth the truth! Cutting in its intensity, this series will show you how the Word of the Lord will render you untouchable when you are aware of your purpose!! Bishop Jordan defines the new breed of people that God is raising up that will know the art of war, understand and love their enemy as they embrace the arms of destiny fulfilled.
4-Video series $80

AUDIO CASSETTE SERIES
BY BISHOP E. BERNARD JORDAN

THE POWER OF INCREASE

This radical tape series by Bishop E. Bernard Jordan clarifies the principles of God that will bring increase into your life. For those who seem that they are in a continual financial rut, this series will place keys of deliverance that will thrust you into true prosperity.
4-Tape audio series $20

FROM BITTER TO BETTER

Everyone that has ever attained a measure of success has endured the gall of bitterness. There are many individuals whose current situations offend the very essence of their sense of righteousness. Yet God, in His sovereignty, will cause all things to work together for their good, since they are "the called of the Lord." Like Joseph, who endured rejection by his family, slavery, false accusation and imprisonment before he attained His purpose in God, so shall we tread upon the steps of adversity as we climb to the pinnacle of success. This series will thrust you into another dimension in God.
4-Tape audio series $20

KINGDOM FINANCES

How are Christians sup-posed to prosper as their soul prospers? What is the mindset of success? This series explores the power of money and the responsi-bility of the Christian to wield his power wisely as an example of good stew-ardship. These tapes are highly recommended for anyone who has had difficulty maintaining a Godly standard in money management 12-Tape audio series $55

THE FAMILY

The various pres-sures of corrupt societal influences have challenged the basic structure of the family. Bishop Jordan gives Scriptural premise for the line of authority that should exist in each family, and the development of healthy relationships. An extensive study, this series will revo-lutionize your home when diligently fol-lowed. 4-Tape audio series $20

PRAYER AND FASTING

The significance of prayer and fasting is discussed in this series. The many facets of prayer are discussed, as well as the mechanics of fasting and opti-mum results, both physically and spiritually. This series is a must for those who wish to develop their spiritual senses to a greater degree.
4-Tape audio series $20
ALSO AVAILABLE IN BOOK

THE HOLY SPIRIT

Is there such a thing as "The Baptism of the Holy Ghost?" "Am I still saved if I don't speak in tongues? What is the pur-pose of tongues? This series gives a detailed explana-tion of the identity and purpose of the Holy Spirit in the life of the believer.
2-Tape audio series $10
ALSO AVAILABLE IN BOOK

BOOKS
BY BISHOP E. BERNARD JORDAN

THE MAKING OF THE DREAM
Are you riding the waves to an unknown shore? Is God's will passing you by? Is your God-given vision a dream or a reality? If you aren't sure of your life's destination then you need to hear "The Making of the Dream!" These teachings are remarkable because they will assist you in establishing workable goals in pursuit of success. You God-given dream will no longer be incomprehensible, but it will be touchable, believable and conceivable! $10

THE SCIENCE OF PROPHECY
A clear, concise and detailed exposition on the prophetic ministry and addresses many misnomers and misunderstandings concerning the ministry of the New Testament prophet. If you have any questions concerning prophetic ministry, or would like to receive sound, scriptural teachings on this subject, this book is for you! $10

MENTORING: THE MISSING LINK
Deals with the necessity of proper nurturing in the things of God by divinely appointed and anointed individuals placed in the lives of potential leaders. God's structure of authority and protocol for the purpose of the maturation of effective leadership is thoroughly discussed and explained. This book is highly recommended for anyone who believes that God has called them to any type of ministry in the Body of Christ. $10

MEDITATION: THE KEY TO NEW HORIZONS IN GOD
Designed to help you unlock the inner dimensions of Scripture in your pursuit of the knowledge of God. Long considered exclusively in the domain of New Age and eastern religions, meditation is actually part of the heritage of Christians, and is to be an essential part of every believer's life. We have been given a mandate to meditate upon the Word of God in order to effect prosperity and wholeness in our lives. This book gives some foundational principles to stimulate our transformation into the express image of Jesus Christ. $10

PROPHETIC GENESIS

Explores the realms of the genesis of prophecy...the beginning of God communicating to mankind. The prophetic ministry is examined in a greater depth, and the impact of various areas such as culture and music upon prophecy are taught in-depth. The prophetic ministry must always operate under proper authority, and this factor is also delved into. This book is designed for the mature student who is ready to enter into new dimensions of the prophetic realm.　$10

THE JOSHUA GENERATION

A book that rings with the sound of confrontation, as the Body of Christ is urged to awaken from passivity to embrace the responsibility to fulfill the mandate of God in this hour! The Joshua Generation is targeted for those who are ready to look beyond the confines of tradition to tackle the weight of change. Are you a pioneer at heart? Then you are a part of The Joshua Generation!! This book is for you!!　$10

SPIRITUAL PROTOCOL

Addresses an excruciating need for order and discipline in the Body of Christ. By aggressively attacking the trend of independence and lawlessness that permeates the Church, the issue of governmental authority and accountability is thoroughly discussed. This manual clearly identifies the delineation of areas and levels of ministry, and brings a fresh understanding of authority and subsequent submission, and their implications for leadership within the House of the Lord. This is a comprehensive study that includes Bishop Jordan's earlier book, Mentoring, and is highly recommended for anyone desiring to understand and align himself with God's order for the New Testament Church.　$10

PRAISE AND WORSHIP

An extensive manual designed to give Scriptural foundation to the ministry of the worshipping arts (musical, dramatic, artistic, literary, oratory, meditative and liturgical dance) in the House of the Lord. The arts are the outward mode of expression of an internal relationship with God, and are employed by God as an avenue through which He will speak and display His Word, and by man as a loving response to the touch of God upon his life. This book will compel the reader to deepen his relationship with his Creator, and explore new degrees of intimacy with our Lord and Saviour, Jesus Christ.　$20

BREAKING SOUL TIES AND GENERATIONAL CURSES

The sins of the father will often attempt to visit this present genera-tion...however, those who understand their authority in Christ can refuse that visitation!! This series reveals the methods of identifying soul ties and curses that attempt to reduplicate themselves generation after generation. If you can point to a recurrent blight within your family lin-eage, such as premature death, familial diseases (alcoholism, diabetes, cancer, divorce, etc., then YOU NEED THIS SERIES!!!

Volume I .... 8-tape series.................$40.00
Volume II .... 8-tape series.................$40.00

WRITTEN JUDGMENTS VOLUME I

Chronicles the Word of the Lord concerning the nations of the world and the Body of Christ at large. Many subjects are addressed, such as the U.S. economy, the progress of the Church, the rise and fall of cer-tain nations, and Bishop Jordan prophecies over every state in America with the exception of Ohio. This is not written for sensationalism, but to challenge the Body of Christ to begin to pray concerning the changes that are to come. $10

WRITTEN JUDGMENTS VOLUME II

A continuation of the Word of the Lord expressed towards the Middle East, the Caribbean nations, America, and the Body of Christ at large. Addresses various issues confronting America, such as abortion, racism, economics and homelessness. A powerful reflection of the judgements of God, which come to effect redemption and reconciliation in the lives of mankind. $10

MINI BOOKS

1. The Purpose of Tongues $1.00
2. Above All Things Get Wisdom...................$1.00
3. Calling Forth The Men of Valor....................$1.00

SCHOOL OF THE PROPHETS
CORRESPONDENCE COURSE

SCHOOL OF THE PROPHETS IS
<u>NOW ON VIDEO</u>

Perhaps you are unable to attend a session of School of the

Prophets as it is held around the nation. Or maybe, you're

an alumnus and you'd just like to review the course again

in the privacy of your own home. Then this set of nine (9)

videos was made just for you!!! Here's what you will

receive when you order TODAY:

- 9 (nine) videos with the entire
  School of the Prophets teaching

- 1 (one) 60-minute audio cassette

- 1 (one) School of the Prophets textbook.

All this for ONLY **$495.**

Special Alumni price **$195**

(800) 4-PROPHET
to order by Credit Card.
All others Use Order Form.

ADDITIONAL VIDEO / AUDIO CASSETTES

This Time Next Year .... 2 videos - $40.00

Prophetic Connection .... 4 videos - $80.00

The Power of Money .... 8 videos - $160.0

Corporate Destiny .... 4 videos - $80.00

The Anointing .... 4 videos - $80.00

The Spirit of the Oppressor - expanded .... 4 videos - $80.00

Boaz & Ruth .... 4 videos - $80.00

How to Train Up A Child .... 4 videos - $80.00

The Power of Oneness .... 4 videos - $80.00

Laws and Principles of the Kingdom .... Vol. I & 2 - $80.00

Spiritual Protocol (Audio) .... 4 tapes   - $40.00

Order Now by Credit Card
and receive 50%
off your total order

or

order by Check or Money order
and receive 40% off.

ORDER FORM

ZOE MINISTRIES
Church Street Station • P.O. Box 270 • New York, NY 10008-0270
212-316-2177 • Fax: 212-316-5769
Visit me on the internet — www.bishopjordan.com

TITLE	QTY	DONATION	TOTAL

Guarantee: You may return any defective item within 90 days for replacement. All offers are subject to change without notice. Please allow 4 weeks for delivery. No COD orders accepted. Make checks payable to ZOE MINISTRIES.

Subtotal	
Shipping	
Donation	
TOTAL	

Name: _____Phone _____

Address: _____

_____Zip _____

Payment by: Check or Money Order (Payable to Zoe Ministries)
Visa • MasterCard • American Express • Discover
Card No.: _____ Exp. Date)_____

Signature (Required) _____